Poetry Builders

Henry and Hala Build a

HAIKU

by Nadia Higgins
illustrated by Brian Caleb Dumm

Content Consultant
Kris Bigalk
Director of Creative Writing
Normandale Community College

NORWOOD HOUSE ■ PRESS
CHICAGO, ILLINOIS

Norwood House Press
P.O. Box 316598
Chicago, Illinois 60631
For information regarding Norwood House Press,
please visit our website at:
www.norwoodhousepress.com or call 866-565-2900.

Editor: Melissa York
Designer: Emily Love
Project Management: Red Line Editorial

Library of Congress Cataloging-in-Publication Data
Higgins, Nadia.
  Henry and Hala build a haiku / by Nadia Higgins ; illustrated
by Brian Dumm.
      p. cm. -- (Poetry builders)
  Includes bibliographical references.
  Summary: "While on a family camping trip, Hala teaches her
friend Henry how to write Haiku, an ancient form of Japanese
poetry. Includes creative writing exercises to assist the reader
in writing haiku"--Provided by publisher.
  ISBN-13: 978-1-59953-435-0 (lib. ed. : alk. paper)
  ISBN-10: 1-59953-435-5 (lib. ed. : alk. paper)
 1. Haiku, American. 2. Children's poetry, American. 3. Children's poetry--Authorship. I. Dumm, Brian Caleb, ill. II. Title.
  PS3608.I3665H46 2011
  811'.54--dc22
                            2010043866

Words in **black bold** are defined in the glossary.

"Why I Love to Write Poems"

I love to write poems because I have a lot to say. I take my notebook everywhere to write down what I see. I want to share my thoughts and feelings. Sometimes, I just write in my diary. But poetry helps me describe some things even better.

When I write a poem, I don't just think about what the words mean. I think about how they sound. I have fun playing with words! Sometimes I try to sing them. Sometimes I clap along!

We have been learning about haiku poems in school. Haiku is an old form of Japanese poetry. Haiku poems are very, very short. And they don't **rhyme**. My teacher, Miss Lyric, says that's why a lot of people think haiku poems are easy. But those teensy-weensy poems are hard! You only get a few words to say what you want! So every word has to be good.

Wow, I have written a lot about poems! Like Miss Lyric says, it's easy to write about something you love.

By Hala, age 10

Hanging above me
Henry in his string cocoon—
When will he come out?

"Henry! . . . Ouch!" Hala bumped her head as she jumped up. "Henry!" Hala grabbed the edge of Henry's hammock and shook it.

"Hmmmmmmm?" Henry's eyes opened halfway.

"I finished my haiku!" Hala waved her notebook in front of Henry's face. "Want to read it? It's about you!"

Henry yawned. He scratched an ear. "Hi-what?"

"Haiku, Henry! An old form of Japanese poetry. Simple, little poems . . ." As Hala explained, she made giant circles with her arms. "Tiny celebrations of nature, the seasons, and ordinary things—"

"Let me see what's so exciting." Henry sat up. Hala handed Henry her notebook, and he started reading.

Hala sat down on the grass and hugged her knees. Beyond the hill, the lake was sparkling. The cool grass tickled her toes. She breathed in the sharp, sweet smell of campfires. It was the kind of day that could make a kid want to write a poem.

Henry jumped out of his hammock. The
notebook went flying. "Whoooosh." He
bopped up and down, flapping his arms.
"Whooosh. Whoosh."

Hala laughed and picked up her notebook. "The butterfly came out of its cocoon!"

"No, a robotic bat with laser claws!" Henry clawed at an imaginary enemy. "Whoooosh." Henry flew over to Hala. "Write another one!" he said.

"No, you try it," Hala said.

"Okay . . ." Henry began. "Once there was a bat, a mean, mean robotic bat with poisonous teeth and laser claws—"

"Whoa—stop!" Hala said. "That's too many **syllables**!"

"Huh?" Henry stopped flapping.

"You know, a syllable—like a **beat** in a word. Hen-ry. Two syllables. Poi-son-ous. Three."

"Ro-bot-ic bat—four!" Henry said.

"A haiku has just 17 syllables. It goes 5-7-5: Five syllables on the first line, seven on the second, and five on the third. See?"

They counted the syllables in Hala's haiku. Hala tapped her foot with each beat. Henry flapped some more.

Hang-ing a-bove me
Hen-ry in his string co-coon—
When will he come out?

Hala turned the page. "A haiku doesn't rhyme, either. Want to see some more?" The two friends took turns marking the beats on Hala's poems.

tiny rivers crawl
zigzagging down my window—
raindrops are racing!

Mado and Misha
whispering by the lockers
Did I hear my name?

My red balloon—whoops!
Up, up, up, smaller, smaller—
Erased by the sky

Watermelon slice
curved triangle, sweet and pink
My sister laughing

Folded, packed, checked, zipped,
washed, buttoned, and organized—
School starts tomorrow!

Outside, a car—whoosh!
Light slithers around my room.
Where is it going?

rock on the sidewalk
white circle, smooth, warm, perfect
a sun in my hand

the cat slips past me—
a black thread unraveling
into the black night

purple hula hoop
around and around and ar—
start over again.

"That's my favorite one," Henry said, pointing. "The one that says, 'Erased by the sky!'" This time, he held his arms out straight and went "Vrrrrrrrr" instead of "Whooosh."

"I'm a supersonic jet

I'm the best

I'm—"

Henry stopped. "Hala, this is hard!"

"I know!" Hala said. "C'mon. I have an idea." She led him to the lake.

"A haiku is supposed to surprise you, Henry." Hala dropped at the hill and rolled down. "Delight you, amaze you!"

Henry rolled after her. "It doesn't just tell about something?" he asked at the bottom.

"No!" Hala said. "It also paints a picture."

Hala took the notebook from Henry and ripped out a sheet. Then she handed the notebook back to him. She pulled a pencil from behind her ear and started writing. "Just write, Henry. Make a list of everything you notice."

When they were done, they showed each other their lists.

Hala:
lake has a million tiny ripples
canoe slices the ripples
sand grains sparkle on my skin
Henry's sunscreen smells like lemons
cattails look like fuzzy brown hot dogs
minnows tickle my feet

Henry:
mosquito buzzing
slimy, green rock
Hala's pencil making scratchy noises
teenagers laughing
white seagulls on blue sky
noisy seagulls—squaaaaawk!
dragonfly wings are see-through
sand in my underwear

Next, Henry and Hala looked over their lists. Each picked their favorite thing. Hala's was sand grains. Henry's was seagulls. They started writing.

"What do you think of this, Hala?" Henry showed her a first **draft** of his poem.

Seagulls flying everywhere
They look like they are chasing each other
Squaaaaaaawk! Why are they yelling?

Henry knew he had too many syllables. Hala liked the second line. "Your haiku makes me think of recess," she said. That gave Henry an idea.

Meanwhile, Hala kept working on her notes. "What do you think?"

sparkling on my skin
red, brown, yellow grains of sand
each its own haiku

"Cool!" Then Henry turned back to his notebook. He erased, then wrote some more, then erased. Finally, he shot up. "Look!"

swooping and dodging
seagulls calling out: squaaaaaawk, squaaaaaawk
"Just try and catch me!"

"Squaaaaaaawk!" Henry yelled. With that, Henry was off again, arms flapping.

"Great haiku, Henry!" Hala called, flapping after him. In her mind, she added more items to her list, storing them away for her next haiku:

flying with Henry
green grass blurry under my feet
heart pounding
hair blowing in the wind
FUN FUN FUN!

You Can Write a Haiku, too!

A haiku does not rhyme. It has three lines. A haiku has 17 syllables: 5 in line one, 7 in line two, and 5 in line three. A haiku can be about anything you want, but a lot of times haiku poems are about nature, the seasons, and ordinary things.

Making lists is a great way to start writing a haiku. First, think of a subject. You could write about your favorite animal, your best friend, your favorite food, or anything else you love. Let's start with pizza.

Think of some words that describe what that thing is like or what it makes you think about.

Hot triangle
pepperoni makes polka dots
gooey cheese
Yummmmm!
We always have pizza after soccer games
Cozy
Eeeeewey mushrooms I have to pick off

Now, put it all together. Don't worry about the syllables at first. Start with your favorite item from the list. Then, start writing. You may use other items from your list. Or, as you write, new ideas will probably come to you. Don't be afraid to cross out or start over.

Once you are happy with your ideas, you can focus on syllables. What words can you cut? What words can you swap out with other ones to make your poem go 5-7-5?

Here's a draft. It goes 7-6-9.

Hot, gooey, cheesy pizza
I can't wait to eat it
I hope Mom didn't order mushrooms

See what happens when it's changed to 5-7-5?

Hot, gooey pizza
I can't wait to take a bite—
But no mushrooms, please!

Glossary

beat: the pattern of a poem's rhythm.

draft: an early try at writing a poem. Poets may write many drafts to create a finished poem.

rhyme: a word that shares the end sounds of another word but has a different beginning—like dust, must, rust, and fussed.

syllables: the bits of sound that make up a word. Each syllable must have a vowel sound. Sometimes the vowel has some consonants with it. *Word* has one syllable. *Syllable* has three—syl-la-ble.

For More Information

Books

Clements, Andrew. *Dogku*. New York: Simon and Schuster, 2007.

Keisuke Nishimoto. *Haiku Picturebook for Children*. Torrance, CA: Heian International, 2008.

Raczka, Bob. *Guyku: A Year of Haiku for Boys*. New York: Houghton Mifflin, 2010.

Websites

Fern's Poetry Club
pbskids.org/arthur/games/poetry/what.html
The characters of the PBS program "Arthur" teach all about different types of poetry.

Two Dragonflies: Haiku and Music for Children
www.twodragonflies.com/
This website includes classic haiku, haiku for children, and haiku written by children.

About the Author

Nadia Higgins is a children's book writer in Minneapolis, Minnesota. Her favorite poem for kids is "I'M alL MIxED uP" by Jack Prelutsky. She reads at least one poem every day with her two daughters.

About the Illustrator

Brian Caleb Dumm is a professional illustrator and art educator from Pennsylvania.